THE BEST OF
RUDYARD KIPLING

A COLLECTION OF
ESSENTIAL POETRY

By

RUDYARD KIPLING

Read &' Co.

Copyright © 2020 Ragged Hand

This edition is published by Ragged Hand,
an imprint of Read & Co.

This book is copyright and may not be reproduced or copied in any
way without the express permission of the publisher in writing.

British Library Cataloguing-in-Publication Data
A catalogue record for this book is available
from the British Library.

Read & Co. is part of Read Books Ltd.
For more information visit
www.readandcobooks.co.uk

CONTENTS

Rudyard Kipling

A British author who was born in Bombay on the 30th of December 1865. His father, John Lockwood Kipling (1837–1911), an artist of considerable ability, was from 1875 to 1893 curator of the Lahore museum in India. His mother was Miss Alice Macdonald of Birmingham, two of whose sisters were married respectively to Sir E. Burne-Jones and Sir Edward Poynter. He was educated at the United Services College, Westward Ho, North Devon, of which a somewhat lurid account is given in his story *Staley and Co.* On his return to India he became at the age of seventeen the sub-editor of the Lahore *Civil and Military Gazette.*

In 1886, in his twenty-first year, he published *Departmental Ditties*, a volume of light verse chiefly satirical, only in two or three poems giving promise of his authentic poetical note. In 1887 he published *Plain Tales from the Hills*, a collection mainly of the stories contributed to his own journal. During the next two years he brought out, in six slim paper-covered volumes of Wheeler's Railway Library (Allahabad), *Soldiers Three, The Story of the Gadsbys, In Black and White, Under the Deodars, The Phantom 'Rickshaw* and *Wee Willie Winkee*, at a rupee apiece. These were in form and substance a continuation of the *Plain Tales.* This series of tales all written before the author was twenty-four, revealed a new master of fiction. A few, but those the best, he afterwards said that his father gave him. The rest were the harvest of his own powers of observation vitalized by imagination. In method they owed something to Bret Harte; in matter and spirit they were absolutely original.

They were unequal, as his books continued to be throughout; the sketches of Anglo-Indian social life being generally inferior to the rest. The style was to some extent disfigured by jerkiness and mannered tricks. But Mr Kipling possessed the supreme spell of the story-teller to entrance and transport. The freshness of the invention, the variety of character, the vigour of narrative, the raciness of dialogue, the magic of atmosphere, were alike remarkable. The soldier-stories, especially the exuberant vitality of the cycle which contains the immortal Mulvaney, established the author's fame throughout the world. The child-stories and tales of the British official were not less masterly, while the tales of native life and of adventure "beyond the pale" disclosed an even finer and deeper vein of romance.

India, which had been an old story for generations of Englishmen, was revealed in these brilliant pictures as if seen for the first time in its variety, colour and passion, vivid as mirage, enchanting as the *Arabian Nights*. The new author's talent was quickly recognized in India, but it was not till the books reached England that his true rank was appreciated and proclaimed.

Between 1887 and 1889 he travelled through India, China, Japan and America, finally arriving in England to find himself already famous. His travel sketches, contributed to *The Civil and Military Gazette* and *The Pioneer*, were afterwards collected (the author's hand having been forced by unauthorized publication) in the two volumes *From Sea to Sea* (1899). A further set of Indian tales, equal to the best, appeared in *Macmillan's Magazine* and were republished with others in *Life's Handicap* (1891). In *The Light that Failed* (1891, after appearing with a different ending in *Lippincott's Magazine*). Mr Kipling essayed his first long story (dramatized 1905), but with comparative unsuccess.

In his subsequent work his delight in the display of descriptive and verbal technicalities grew on him. His polemic against "the sheltered life" and "little Englandism" became more didactic. His terseness sometimes degenerated into abruptness and obscurity. But in the meanwhile his genius became prominent in verse.

Readers of the *Plain Tales* had been impressed by the snatches of poetry prefixed to them for motto, certain of them being subscribed "Barrack Room Ballad" Mr Kipling now contributed to the *National Observer*, then edited by W. E. Henley, a series of *Barrack Room Ballads*. These vigorous verses in soldier slang, when published in a book in 1892, together with the fine ballad of "East and West" and other poems, won for their author a second fame, wider than he had attained as a story-teller. In this volume the Ballads of the "Bolivar" and of the "Clampherdown," introducing Mr Kipling's poetry of the ocean and the engine-room, and "The Flag of England," finding a voice for the Imperial sentiment, which—largely under the influence of Mr Kipling's own writings—had been rapidly gaining force in England, gave the key-note of much of his later verse.

In 1898 Mr Kipling paid the first of several visits to South Africa and became imbued with a type of imperialism that reacted on his literature, not altogether to its advantage. Before finally settling in England Mr Kipling lived some years in America and married in 1892 Miss Caroline Starr Balestier, sister of the Wolcott Balestier to whom he dedicated *Barrack Room Ballads*, and with whom in collaboration he wrote the *Naulahka* (1891), one of his less successful books. The next collection of stories, *Many Inventions* (1893), contained the splendid Mulvaney extravaganza, "My Lord the Elephant"; a vividly realized tale of metempsychosis, "The Finest Story in the World"; and in that fascinating tale "In the Rukh," the prelude to the next new exhibition of the author's genius. This came in 1894 with The *Jungle Book*, followed in 1895 by *The Second Jungle Book*. With these inspired beast-stories Kipling conquered a new world and a new audience, and produced what many critics regard as his most flawless work.

His chief subsequent publications were *The Seven Seas* (poems), 1896; *Captains Courageous* (a yarn of deep-sea fishery), 1897; *The Day's Work* (collected stories), 1898; *A Fleet in Being* (an account of a cruise in a man-of-war), 1898; *Stalky and Co.* (mentioned above), 1899; *From Sea to Sea* (mentioned above),1899; *Kim*, 1901; *Just So Stories* (for children), 1902; *The*

Five Nations (poems, concluding with what proved Mr Kipling's most universally known and popular poem, "Recessional," originally published in *The Times* on the 17th of July 1897 on the occasion of Queen Victoria's second jubilee), 1903; *Traffics and Discoveries* (collected stories), 1904; *Puck of Pook's Hill* (stories), 1906; *Actions and Reactions* (stories), 1909. Of these Kim was notable as far the most successful of Mr Kipling's longer narratives, though it is itself rather in the nature of a string of episodes. But everything he wrote, even to a farcical extravaganza inspired by his enthusiasm for the motor-car, breathed the meteoric energy that was the nature of the man.

A vigorous and unconventional poet, a pioneer in the modern phase of literary Imperialism, and one of the rare masters in English prose of the art of the short story, Mr Kipling had already by the opening of the 20th century won the most conspicuous place among the creative literary forces of his day. His position in English literature was recognized in 1907 by the award to him of the Nobel prize.

A BIOGRAPHY FROM
1911 *Encyclopædia Britannica, Volume 15*

THE BEST OF
RUDYARD KIPLING

A COLLECTION OF ESSENTIAL POETRY

GUNGA DIN

You may talk o' gin and beer
When you're quartered safe out 'ere,
An' you're sent to penny-fights an' Aldershot it;
But when it comes to slaughter
You will do your work on water,
An' you'll lick the bloomin' boots of 'im that's got it.
Now in Injia's sunny clime,
Where I used to spend my time
A-servin' of 'Er Majesty the Queen,
Of all them blackfaced crew
The finest man I knew
Was our regimental bhisti[1], Gunga Din.
    He was"Din! Din! Din!
  "You limpin' lump o' brick-dust, Gunga Din!
    "Hi! Slippy *hitherao!*[2]
     "Water, get it! *Panee lao*[3]
  "You squidgy-nosed old idol, Gunga Din."

The uniform 'e wore
Was nothin' much before,
An' rather less than 'arf o' that be'ind,
For a piece o' twisty rag
An' a goatskin water-bag
Was all the field-equipment 'e could find.
When the sweatin' troop-train lay
In a sidin' through the day,
Where the 'eat would make your bloomin' eyebrows crawl,
We shouted" Harry By![4]"
Till our throats were bricky-dry,

Then we wopped 'im 'cause 'e couldn't serve us all.
    It was"Din! Din! Din!
   "You 'eathen, where the mischief 'ave you been?
     "You put some *juldee*[5] in it
     "Or I'll *marrow*[6] you this minute
    "If you don't fill up my helmet, Gunga Din!"

'E would dot an' carry one
Till the longest day was done;
An' 'e didn't seem to know the use o' fear.
If we charged or broke or cut,
You could bet your bloomin' nut,
'E'd be waitin' fifty paces right flank rear.
With 'is mussick' on 'is back,
'E would skip with our attack,
An' watch us till the bugles made"Retire,"
An' for all 'is dirty 'ide
'E was white, clear white, inside
When 'e went to tend the wounded under fire!
    It was"Din! Din! Din!"
  With the bullets kickin' dust-spots on the green
    When the cartridges ran out,
     You could hear the front-ranks shout,
  "Hi! ammunition-mules an' Gunga Din!"

I sha'n't forgit the night
When I dropped be'ind the fight
With a bullet where my belt-plate should 'a' been.
I was chokin' mad with thirst,
An' the man that spied me first
Was our good old grinnin', gruntin' Gunga Din.
'E lifted up my 'ead,
An' he plugged me where I bled, An' 'e
guv me 'arf-a-pint o' water green.
It was crawlin' and it stunk,

But of all the drinks I've drunk,
I'm gratefullest to one from Gunga Din.
It was"Din! Din! Din!
"'Ere's a beggar with a bullet through 'is spleen"
"'E's chawin' up the ground,
"An' 'e's kickin' all around:
"For Gawd's sake git the water, Gunga Din!

'E carried me away
To where a dooli lay,
An' a bullet come an' drilled the beggar clean.
'E put me safe inside,
An' just before 'e died,
"I 'ope you liked your drink" sez Gunga Din.
So I'll meet 'im later on
At the place where 'e is gone
Where it's always double drill and no canteen.
'E'll be squattin' on the coals
Givin' drink to poor damned souls,
An' I'll get a swig in hell from Gunga Din!
Yes, Din! Din! Din!
You Lazarushian-leather Gunga Din!
Though I've belted you and flayed you,
By the livin' Gawd that made you,
You're a better man than I am, Gunga Din!

FOOTNOTES

[1] water-carrier
[2] come here
[3] bring water
[4] O Brother
[5] quickly
[6] hit

IF—

If you can keep your head when all about you
    Are losing theirs and blaming it on you,
If you can trust yourself when all men doubt you,
    But make allowance for their doubting too;
If you can wait and not be tired by waiting,
    Or being lied about, don't deal in lies,
Or being hated, don't give way to hating,
    And yet don't look too good, nor talk too wise:

If you can dream—and not make dreams your master;
    If you can think—and not make thoughts your aim;
If you can meet with Triumph and Disaster
    And treat those two impostors just the same;
If you can bear to hear the truth you've spoken
    Twisted by knaves to make a trap for fools,
Or watch the things you gave your life to, broken,
    And stoop and build 'em up with worn-out tools:

If you can make one heap of all your winnings
    And risk it on one turn of pitch-and-toss,
And lose, and start again at your beginnings
    And never breathe a word about your loss;
If you can force your heart and nerve and sinew
    To serve your turn long after they are gone,
And so hold on when there is nothing in you
    Except the Will which says to them: 'Hold on!'

If you can talk with crowds and keep your virtue,
    Or walk with Kings—nor lose the common touch,
If neither foes nor loving friends can hurt you,
    If all men count with you, but none too much;
If you can fill the unforgiving minute
    With sixty seconds' worth of distance run,
Yours is the Earth and everything that's in it,
    And—which is more—you'll be a Man, my son!

RECESSIONAL

1897

God of our fathers, known of old,
   Lord of our far-flung battle-line,
Beneath whose awful Hand we hold
   Dominion over palm and pine—
Lord God of Hosts, be with us yet,
Lest we forget—lest we forget!

The tumult and the shouting dies;
   The Captains and the Kings depart:
Still stands Thine ancient sacrifice,
   An humble and a contrite heart.
Lord God of Hosts, be with us yet,
Lest we forget—lest we forget!

Far-called, our navies melt away;
   On dune and headland sinks the fire:
Lo, all our pomp of yesterday
   Is one with Nineveh and Tyre!
Judge of the Nations, spare us yet,
Lest we forget—lest we forget!

If, drunk with sight of power, we loose
   Wild tongues that have not Thee in awe,
Such boastings as the Gentiles use,
   Or lesser breeds without the Law—
Lord God of Hosts, be with us yet,
Lest we forget—lest we forget!

For heathen heart that puts her trust
    In reeking tube and iron shard,
All valiant dust that builds on dust,
    And guarding, calls not Thee to guard,
For frantic boast and foolish word—
Thy mercy on Thy People, Lord!

THE GODS OF THE COPYBOOK HEADINGS

AS I PASS through my incarnations in every age and race,
I make my proper prostrations to the Gods of the Market Place.
Peering through reverent fingers I watch them flourish and fall,
And the Gods of the Copybook Headings, I notice, outlast them all.

We were living in trees when they met us. They showed us each in turn
That Water would certainly wet us, as Fire would certainly burn:
But we found them lacking in Uplift, Vision and Breadth of Mind,
So we left them to teach the Gorillas while we followed the March
 of Mankind.

We moved as the Spirit listed. They never altered their pace,
Being neither cloud nor wind-borne like the Gods of the Market Place,
But they always caught up with our progress, and presently word
 would come
That a tribe had been wiped off its icefield, or the lights had gone
 out in Rome.

With the Hopes that our World is built on they were utterly out of touch,
They denied that the Moon was Stilton; they denied she was even Dutch;
They denied that Wishes were Horses; they denied that a Pig had Wings;
So we worshipped the Gods of the Market Who promised these
 beautiful things.

When the Cambrian measures were forming, They promised
  perpetual peace.
They swore, if we gave them our weapons, that the wars of the
  tribes would cease.
But when we disarmed They sold us and delivered us bound to our foe,
And the Gods of the Copybook Headings said: "*Stick to the Devil you know.*"

On the first Feminian Sandstones we were promised the Fuller Life
(Which started by loving our neighbour and ended by loving his wife)
Till our women had no more children and the men lost reason and faith,
And the Gods of the Copybook Headings said: "*The Wages of Sin is Death.*"

In the Carboniferous Epoch we were promised abundance for all,
By robbing selected Peter to pay for collective Paul;
But, though we had plenty of money, there was nothing our
  money could buy,
And the Gods of the Copybook Headings said: "*If you don't work you die.*"

Then the Gods of the Market tumbled, and their smooth-tongued
  wizards withdrew
And the hearts of the meanest were humbled and began to believe it was true
That All is not Gold that Glitters, and Two and Two make Four
And the Gods of the Copybook Headings limped up to explain it once more.

As it will be in the future, it was at the birth of Man
There are only four things certain since Social Progress began.
That the Dog returns to his Vomit and the Sow returns to her Mire,
And the burnt Fool's bandaged finger goes wabbling back to the Fire;
And that after this is accomplished, and the brave new world begins
When all men are paid for existing and no man must pay for his sins,
As surely as Water will wet us, as surely as Fire will burn,
The Gods of the Copybook Headings with terror and slaughter return!

THE WHITE MAN'S BURDEN

TAKE up the White Man's burden—
Send forth the best ye breed—
Go bind your sons to exile
To serve your captives' need;
To wait in heavy harness
On fluttered folk and wild—
Your new-caught sullen peoples,
Half devil and half child.

Take up the White Man's burden—
In patience to abide
To veil the threat of terror
And check the show of pride;
By open speech and simple,
An hundred times made plain,
To seek another's profit,
And work another's gain.

Take up the White Man's burden—
The savage wars of peace—
Fill full the mouth of famine
And bid the sickness cease;
And when your goal is nearest
The end for others sought,
Watch Sloth and heathen Folly
Bring all your hopes to nought.

Take up the White Man's burden—
No tawdry rule of kings,
But toil of serf and sweeper—
The tale of common things.
The ports ye shall not enter,
The roads ye shall not tread,
Go make them with your living,
And mark them with your dead!

Take up the White Man's burden—
And reap his old reward,
The blame of those ye better,
The hate of those ye guard—
The cry of hosts ye humour
(Ah slowly!) towards the light—
"Why brought ye us from bondage,
"Our loved Egyptian night ?"

Take up the White Man's burden—
Ye dare not stoop to less—
Nor call too loud on Freedom
To cloak your weariness;
By all ye cry or whisper,
By all ye leave or do,
The silent sullen peoples
Shall weigh your Gods and you.

Take up the White Man's burden—
Have done with childish days—
The lightly proffered laurel,
The easy, ungrudged praise.
Comes now, to search your manhood
Through all the thankless years,
Cold-edged with dear-bought wisdom,
The judgement of your peers.

MESOPOTAMIA

1917

They shall not return to us, the resolute, the young,
  The eager and whole-hearted whom we gave:
But the men who left them thriftily to die in their own dung,
  Shall they come with years and honour to the grave?

They shall not return to us, the strong men coldly slain
  In sight of help denied from day to day:
But the men who edged their agonies and chid them in their pain,
  Are they too strong and wise to put away?

Our dead shall not return to us while Day and Night divide—
  Never while the bars of sunset hold.
But the idle-minded overlings who quibbled while they died,
  Shall they thrust for high employments as of old?

Shall we only threaten and be angry for an hour?
  When the storm is ended shall we find
How softly but how swiftly they have sidled back to power
  By the favour and contrivance of their kind?

Even while they soothe us, while they promise large amends,
  Even while they make a show of fear,
Do they call upon their debtors, and take counsel with their friends,
  To conform and re-establish each career?

Their lives cannot repay us—their death could not undo—
    The shame that they have laid upon our race.
But the slothfulness that wasted and the arrogance that slew,
    Shall we leave it unabated in its place?

THE FEMALE
OF THE SPECIES

WHEN the Himalayan peasant meets the he-bear in his pride,
He shouts to scare the monster, who will often turn aside.
But the she-bear thus accosted rends the peasant tooth and nail.
For the female of the species is more deadly than the male.

When Nag the basking cobra hears the careless foot of man,
He will sometimes wriggle sideways and avoid it if he can.
But his mate makes no such motion where she camps beside the trail.
For the female of the species is more deadly than the male.

When the early Jesuit fathers preached to Hurons and Choctaws,
They prayed to be delivered from the vengeance of the squaws.
'Twas the women, not the warriors, turned those stark enthusiasts pale.
For the female of the species is more deadly than the male.

Man's timid heart is bursting with the things he must not say,
For the Woman that God gave him isn't his to give away;
But when hunter meets with husband, each confirms the other's tale—
The female of the species is more deadly than the male.

Man, a bear in most relations—worm and savage otherwise,—
Man propounds negotiations, Man accepts the compromise.
Very rarely will he squarely push the logic of a fact
To its ultimate conclusion in unmitigated act.

Fear, or foolishness, impels him, ere he lay the wicked low,
To concede some form of trial even to his fiercest foe.
Mirth obscene diverts his anger—Doubt and Pity oft perplex
Him in dealing with an issue—to the scandal of The Sex!

But the Woman that God gave him, every fibre of her frame
Proves her launched for one sole issue, armed and engined for the same;
And to serve that single issue, lest the generations fail,
The female of the species must be deadlier than the male.

She who faces Death by torture for each life beneath her breast
May not deal in doubt or pity—must not swerve for fact or jest.
These be purely male diversions—not in these her honour dwells.
She the Other Law we live by, is that Law and nothing else.

She can bring no more to living than the powers that make her great
As the Mother of the Infant and the Mistress of the Mate.
And when Babe and Man are lacking and she strides unclaimed to claim
Her right as femme (and baron), her equipment is the same.

She is wedded to convictions—in default of grosser ties;
Her contentions are her children, Heaven help him who denies!—
He will meet no suave discussion, but the instant, white-hot, wild,
Wakened female of the species warring as for spouse and child.

Unprovoked and awful charges—even so the she-bear fights,
Speech that drips, corrodes, and poisons—even so the cobra bites,
Scientific vivisection of one nerve till it is raw
And the victim writhes in anguish—like the Jesuit with the squaw!

So it comes that Man, the coward, when he gathers to confer
With his fellow-braves in council, dare not leave a place for her
Where, at war with Life and Conscience, he uplifts his erring hands
To some God of Abstract justice—which no woman understands.

And Man knows it! Knows, moreover, that the Woman that God gave him
Must command but may not govern—shall enthral but not enslave him.
And She knows, because She warns him, and Her instincts never fail,
That the Female of Her Species is more deadly than the Male.

THE BALLAD
OF EAST AND WEST

Oh, East is East, and West is West, and never the twain shall meet,
Till Earth and Sky stand presently at God's great Judgment Seat;
But there is neither East nor West, Border, nor Breed, nor Birth,
When two strong men stand face to face, though they come from the
 ends of the earth!

Kamal is out with twenty men to raise the Border side,
And he has lifted the Colonel's mare that is the Colonel's pride.
He has lifted her out of the stable-door between the dawn and day
And turned the calkins upon her feet, and ridden her far away.

Then up and spoke the Colonel's son that led a troop of the Guides
Is there never a man of all my men can say where Kamal hides?"
Then up and spoke Mohammed Khan, the son of the Ressaldar:
"If ye know the track of the morning-mist, ye know where his pickets are.
"At dusk he harries the Abazai - at dawn he is into Bonair,
"But he must go by Fort Bukloh to his own place to fare.
"So if ye gallop to Fort Bukloh as fast as a bird can fly,
"By the favour of God ye may cut him off ere he win to the Tongue of Jagai.
"But if he be past the Tongue of Jagai, right swiftly turn ye then,
"For the length and the breadth of that grisly plain is sown
 with Kamal's men.
"There is rock to the left, and rock to the right, and low lean thorn between,
"And ye may hear a breech-bolt snick where never a man is seen."

27

The Colonel's son has taken horse, and a raw rough dun was he,
With the mouth of a bell and the heart of Hell and the head of a gallows-tree.
The Colonel's son to the Fort has won, they bid him stay to eat
Who rides at the tail of a Border thief, he sits not long at his meat.
He's up and away from Fort Bukloh as fast as he can fly,
Till he was aware of his father's mare in the gut of the Tongue of Jagai,
Till he was aware of his father's mare with Kamal upon her back,
And when he could spy the white of her eye, he made the Pistol crack.
He has fired once, he has fired twice, but the whistling ball went wide.
Ye shoot like a soldier," Kamal said." Show now if ye can ride!
It's up and over the Tongue of Jagai, as blown dust-devils go
The dun he fled like a stag of ten, but the mare like a barren doe.
The dun he leaned against the bit and slugged his head above,
But the red mare played with the snaffle-bars, as a maiden plays with a glove.
There was rock to the left and rock to the right, and low lean thorn between,
And thrice he heard a breech-bolt snick tho' never a man was seen.

They have ridden the low moon out of the sky, their hoofs drum
  up the dawn,
The dun he went like a wounded bull, but the mare like a new-roused fawn.
The dun he fell at a water-course - in a woeful heap fell he,
And Kamal has turned the red mare back, and pulled the rider free.
He has knocked the pistol out of his hand - small room was there to strive,
'Twas only by favour of mine," quoth he," ye rode so long alive:
"There was not a rock for twenty mile, there was not a clump of tree,
"But covered a man of my own men with his rifle cocked on his knee.
"If I had raised my bridle-hand, as I have held it low,
"The little jackals that flee so fast were feasting all in a row.
"If I had bowed my head on my breast, as I have held it high,
"The kite that whistles above us now were gorged till she could not fly."
Lightly answered the Colonel's son:"Do good to bird and beast,
"But count who come for the broken meats before thou makest a feast.
"If there should follow a thousand swords to carry my bones away.
"Belike the price of a jackal's meal were more than a thief could pay.
"They will feed their horse on the standing crop, their men on
  the garnered grain.

28

"The thatch of the byres will serve their fires when all the cattle are slain.
"But if thou thinkest the price be fair - thy brethren wait to sup,
"The hound is kin to the jackal-spawn - howl, dog, and call them up!
"And if thou thinkest the price be high, in steer and gear and stack,
"Give me my father's mare again, and I'll fight my own way back!"

Kamal has gripped him by the hand and set him upon his feet.
"No talk shall be of dogs," said he,"when wolf and grey wolf meet.
"May I eat dirt if thou hast hurt of me in deed or breath;
"What dam of lances brought thee forth to jest at the dawn with Death?"
Lightly answered the Colonel's son:" I hold by the blood of my clan:
Take up the mare for my father's gift - by God, she has carried a man!"
The red mare ran to the Colonel's son, and nuzzled against his breast;
"We be two strong men," said Kamal then," but she loveth the younger best.
"So she shall go with a lifter's dower, my turquoise-studded rein,
"My 'broidered saddle and saddle-cloth, and silver stirrup twain."
The Colonel's son a pistol drew, and held it muzzle-end,
"Ye have taken the one from a foe," said he." Will ye take the mate
  from a friend?"
"A gift for a gift," said Kamal straight;"a limb for the risk of a limb.
"Thy father has sent his son to me, I'll send my son to him!"
With that he whistled his only son, that dropped from a mountain-crest
He trod the ling like a buck in spring, and he looked like a lance in rest.
"Now here is thy master," Kamal said,"who leads a troop of the Guides,
"And thou must ride at his left side as shield on shoulder rides.
"Till Death or I cut loose the tie, at camp and board and bed,
"Thy life is his - thy fate it is to guard him with thy head.
"So, thou must eat the White Queen's meat, and all her foes are thine,
"And thou must harry thy father's hold for the peace of the Border-line.
"And thou must make a trooper tough and hack thy way to power
"Belike they will raise thee to Ressaldar when I am hanged in Peshawur!"

They have looked each other between the eyes, and there they found no fault.
They have taken the Oath of the Brother-in-Blood on leavened
  bread and salt:

They have taken the Oath of the Brother-in-Blood on fire and fresh-cut sod,
On the hilt and the haft of the Khyber knife, and the Wondrous
  Names of God.

The Colonel's son he rides the mare and Kamal's boy the dun,
And two have come back to Fort Bukloh where there went forth but one.
And when they drew to the Quarter-Guard, full twenty swords flew clear
There was not a man but carried his feud with the blood of the mountaineer.
Ha' done! ha' done!" said the Colonel's son." Put up the steel at your sides!
Last night ye had struck at a Border thief - to-night 't is a man of the Guides!"

Oh, East is East, and West is West, and never the twain shall meet,
Till Earth and Sky stand presently at God's great Judgment Seat;
But there is neither East nor West, Border, nor Breed, nor Birth,
When two strong men stand face to face though they come from the
  ends of the earth!

EPITAPHS OF THE WAR

1914-18

"EQUALITY OF SACRIFICE"

A. "I was a Have." B. "I was a 'have-not.'"
(Together) "What hast thou given which I gave not?"

A SERVANT

We were together since the War began.
He was my servant—and the better man.

A SON

My son was killed while laughing at some jest. I would I knew
What it was, and it might serve me in a time when jests are few.

AN ONLY SON

I have slain none except my Mother. She
(Blessing her slayer) died of grief for me.

EX-CLERK

Pity not! The Army gave
Freedom to a timid slave:
In which Freedom did he find
Strength of body, will, and mind:
By which strength he came to prove
Mirth, Companionship, and Love:
For which Love to Death he went:
In which Death he lies content.

THE WONDER

Body and Spirit I surrendered whole
To harsh Instructors—and received a soul . . .
If mortal man could change me through and through
From all I was—what may The God not do?

HINDU SEPOY IN FRANCE

This man in his own country prayed we know not to what Powers.
We pray Them to reward him for his bravery in ours.

THE COWARD

I could not look on Death, which being known,
Men led me to him, blindfold and alone.

SHOCK

My name, my speech, my self I had forgot.
My wife and children came—I knew them not.
I died. My Mother followed. At her call
And on her bosom I remembered all.

A GRAVE NEAR CAIRO

Gods of the Nile, should this stout fellow here
Get out—get out! He knows not shame nor fear.

PELICANS IN THE WILDERNESS

A Grave near Halfa

The blown sand heaps on me, that none may learn
    Where I am laid for whom my children grieve . . .
O wings that beat at dawning, ye return
    Out of the desert to your young at eve!

TWO
CANADIAN MEMORIALS

I

We giving all gained all.
    Neither lament us nor praise.
Only in all things recall,
    It is Fear, not Death that slays.

II

From little towns in a far land we came,
  To save our honour and a world aflame.
By little towns in a far land we sleep;
  And trust that world we won for you to keep!

THE FAVOUR

Death favoured me from the first, well knowing I could not endure
  To wait on him day by day. He quitted my betters and came
Whistling over the fields, and, when he had made all sure,
  "Thy line is at end," he said,"but at least I have saved its name."

THE BEGINNER

On the first hour of my first day
  In the front trench I fell.
(Children in boxes at a play
  Stand up to watch it well.)

R. A. F.
(AGED EIGHTEEN)

Laughing through clouds, his milk-teeth still unshed,
  Cities and men he smote from overhead.
His deaths delivered, he returned to play
  Childlike, with childish things now put away.

THE REFINED MAN

I was of delicate mind. I stepped aside for my needs,
  Disdaining the common office. I was seen from afar and killed . . .
How is this matter for mirth? Let each man be judged by his deeds.
  I have paid my price to live with myself on the terms that I willed.

NATIVE WATER-CARRIER (M. E. F.)

Prometheus brought down fire to men,
  This brought up water.
The Gods are jealous—now, as then,
  Giving no quarter.

BOMBED IN LONDON

On land and sea I strove with anxious care
To escape conscription. It was in the air!

THE SLEEPY SENTINAL

Faithless the watch that I kept: now I have none to keep.
  I was slain because I slept: now I am slain I sleep.
Let no man reproach me again, whatever watch is unkept—
  I sleep because I am slain. They slew me because I slept.

BATTERIES OUT OF AMMUNITION

If any mourn us in the workshop, say
We died because the shift kept holiday.

COMMON FORM

If any question why we died,
Tell them, because our fathers lied.

A DEAD STATESMAN

I could not dig: I dared not rob:
Therefore I lied to please the mob.
Now all my lies are proved untrue
And I must face the men I slew.
What tale shall serve me here among
Mine angry and defrauded young?

THE REBEL

If I had clamoured at Thy Gate
    For gift of Life on Earth,
And, thrusting through the souls that wait,
    Flung headlong into birth—
Even then, even then, for gin and snare
    About my pathway spread,
Lord, I had mocked Thy thoughtful care
    Before I joined the Dead!
But now? . . . I was beneath Thy Hand
    Ere yet the Planets came.
And now—though Planets pass, I stand
    The witness to Thy shame!

THE OBEDIENT

Daily, though no ears attended,
    Did my prayers arise.
Daily, though no fire descended,
    Did I sacrifice.
Though my darkness did not lift,
    Though I faced no lighter odds,
Though the Gods bestowed no gift,
                None the less,
    None the less, I served the Gods!

A DRIFTER OFF TARENTUM

He from the wind-bitten North with ship and companions descended,
    Searching for eggs of death spawned by invisible hulls.
Many he found and drew forth. Of a sudden the fishery ended
    In flame and a clamours breath known to the eye-pecking gulls.

DESTROYER IN COLLISION

For Fog and Fate no charm is found
    To lighten or amend.
I, hurrying to my bride, was drowned—
    Cut down by my best friend.

CONVOY ESCORT

I was a shepherd to fools
  Causelessly bold or afraid.
They would not abide by my rules.
  Yet they escaped. For I stayed.

UNKNOWN FEMALE CORPSE

Headless, lacking foot and hand,
Horrible I come to land.
I beseech all women's sons
Know I was a mother once.

RAPED AND REVENGED

One used and butchered me: another spied
Me broken—for which thing an hundred died.
So it was learned among the heathen hosts
How much a freeborn woman's favour costs.

SALONIKAN GRAVE

I have watched a thousand days
Push out and crawl into night
Slowly as tortoises.
Now I, too, follow these.
It is fever, and not the fight—
Time, not battle,—that slays.

THE BRIDEGROOM

Call me not false, beloved,
  If, from thy scarce-known breast
So little time removed,
  In other arms I rest.

  For this more ancient bride,
Whom coldly I embrace,
  Was constant at my side
Before I saw thy face.

Our marriage, often set—
  By miracle delayed—
At last is consummate,
  And cannot be unmade.

  Live, then, whom Life shall cure,
Almost, of Memory,
  And leave us to endure
Its immortality.

V. A. D.
(MEDITERRANEAN)

Ah, would swift ships had never been, for then we ne'er had found,
These harsh Aegean rocks between, this little virgin drowned,
Whom neither spouse nor child shall mourn, but men she nursed
  through pain
And—certain keels for whose return the heathen look in vain.

ACTORS

On a Memorial Tablet
in Holy Trinity Church, Stratford-on-Avon

We counterfeited once for your disport
  Men's joy and sorrow: but our day has passed.
We pray you pardon all where we fell short—
  Seeing we were your servants to this last.

JOURNALISTS

On a Panel in the Hall of the Institute of Journalists

We have served our day.

THE WAY
THROUGH THE WOODS

THEY shut the road through the woods
Seventy years ago.
Weather and rain have undone it again,
And now you would never know
There was once a road through the woods
Before they planted the trees.
It is underneath the coppice and heath,
And the thin anemones.
Only the keeper sees
That, where the ring-dove broods,
And the badgers roll at ease,
There was once a road through the woods.

Yet, if you enter the woods
Of a summer evening late,
When the night-air cools on the trout-ringed pools
Where the otter whistles his mate,
(They fear not men in the woods,
Because they see so few.)
You will hear the beat of a horse's feet,
And the swish of a skirt in the dew,
Steadily cantering through
The misty solitudes,
As though they perfectly knew
The old lost road through the woods.
But there is no road through the woods.

MOTHER O' MINE

IF I were hanged on the highest hill,
Mother o' mine, O mother o' mine!
I know whose love would follow me still,
Mother o' mine, O mother o' mine!

If I were drowned in the deepest sea,
Mother o' mine, O mother o' mine !
I know whose tears would come down to me,
Mother o' mine, O mother o' mine !

If I were damned of body and soul,
I know whose prayers would make me whole,
Mother o' mine, O mother o' mine!

TOMMY

I WENT into a public 'ouse to get a pint o' beer,
The publican 'e up an' sez," We serve no red-coats here."
The girls be'ind the bar they laughed an' giggled fit to die,
I outs into the street again an' to myself sez I:
O it's Tommy this, an' Tommy that, an'" Tommy, go away";
But it's" Thank you, Mister Atkins," when the band begins to play
The band begins to play, my boys, the band begins to play,
O it's" Thank you, Mister Atkins," when the band begins to play.

I went into a theatre as sober as could be,
They gave a drunk civilian room, but 'adn't none for me;
They sent me to the gallery or round the music-'alls,
But when it comes to fightin', Lord! they'll shove me in the stalls!
For it's Tommy this, an' Tommy that, an'" Tommy, wait outside";
But it's" Special train for Atkins" when the trooper's on the tide
The troopship's on the tide, my boys, the troopship's on the tide,
O it's" Special train for Atkins" when the trooper's on the tide.

Yes, makin' mock o' uniforms that guard you while you sleep
Is cheaper than them uniforms, an' they're starvation cheap.
An' hustlin' drunken soldiers when they're goin' large a bit
Is five times better business than paradin' in full kit.
Then it's Tommy this, an' Tommy that, an` Tommy, 'ow's yer soul?"
But it's" Thin red line of 'eroes" when the drums begin to roll
The drums begin to roll, my boys, the drums begin to roll,
O it's" Thin red line of 'eroes," when the drums begin to roll.

We aren't no thin red 'eroes, nor we aren't no blackguards too,
But single men in barricks, most remarkable like you;
An' if sometimes our conduck isn't all your fancy paints,
Why, single men in barricks don't grow into plaster saints;
While it's Tommy this, an' Tommy that, an` Tommy, fall be'ind,"
But it's" Please to walk in front, sir," when there's trouble in the wind
There's trouble in the wind, my boys, there's trouble in the wind,
O it's" Please to walk in front, sir," when there's trouble in the wind.

You talk o' better food for us, an' schools, an' fires, an' all:
We'll wait for extry rations if you treat us rational.
Don't mess about the cook-room slops, but prove it to our face
The Widow's Uniform is not the soldier-man's disgrace.
For it's Tommy this, an' Tommy that, an` Chuck him out, the brute!"
But it's" Saviour of 'is country" when the guns begin to shoot;
An' it's Tommy this, an' Tommy that, an' anything you please;
An 'Tommy ain't a bloomin' fool — you bet that Tommy sees!

THE GLORY
OF THE GARDEN

OUR England is a garden that is full of stately views,
Of borders, beds and shrubberies and lawns and avenues,
With statues on the terraces and peacocks strutting by;
But the Glory of the Garden lies in more than meets the eye.

For where the old thick laurels grow, along the thin red wall,
You'll find the tool- and potting-sheds which are the heart of all,
The cold-frames and the hot-houses, the dungpits and the tanks,
The rollers, carts and drain-pipes, with the barrows and the planks.

And there you'll see the gardeners, the men and 'Prentice boys
Told off to do as they are bid and do it without noise;
For, except when seeds are planted and we shout to scare the birds,
The Glory of the Garden it abideth not in words.

And some can pot begonias and some can bud a rose,
And some are hardly fit to trust with anything that grows;
But they can roll and trim the lawns and sift the sand and loam,
For the Glory of the Garden occupieth all who come.

Our England is a garden, and such gardens are not made
By singing:—"Oh, how beautiful!" and sitting in the shade,
While better men than we go out and start their working lives
At grubbing weeds from gravel-paths with broken dinnerknives.

There's not a pair of legs so thin, there's not a head so thick,
There's not a hand so weak and white, nor yet a heart so sick,
But it can find some needful job that's crying to be done,
For the Glory of the Garden glorifieth every one.

Then seek your job with thankfulness and work till further orders,
If it's only netting strawberries or killing slugs on borders;
And when your back stops aching and your hands begin to harden,
You will find yourself a partner in the Glory of the Garden.

Oh, Adam was a gardener, and God who made him sees
That half a proper gardener's work is done upon his knees,
So when your work is finished, you can wash your hands and pray
For the Glory of the Garden that it may not pass away!
And the Glory of the Garden it shall never pass away!

DANNY DEEVER

'What are the bugles blowin' for?' said Files-on-Parade.
'To turn you out, to turn you out,' the Colour-Sergeant said.
'What makes you look so white, so white?' said Files-on-Parade.
'I'm dreadin' what I've got to watch,' the Colour-Sergeant said.
For they're hangin' Danny Deever, you can hear the Dead March play,
The Regiment's in 'ollow square—they're hangin' him to-day;
They've taken of his buttons off an' cut his stripes away,
An' they're hangin' Danny Deever in the mornin'.

'What makes the rear-rank breathe so 'ard?' said Files-on-Parade.
'It's bitter cold, it's bitter cold,' the Colour-Sergeant said.
'What makes that front-rank man fall down?' said Files-on-Parade.
'A touch o' sun, a touch o' sun,' the Colour-Sergeant said.
They are hangin' Danny Deever, they are marchin' of 'im round,
They 'ave 'alted Danny Deever by 'is coffin on the ground;
An' 'e'll swing in 'arf a minute for a sneakin' shootin' hound—
O they're hangin' Danny Deever in the mornin'!

''Is cot was right-'and cot to mine,' said Files-on-Parade.
''E's sleepin' out an' far to-night,' the Colour-Sergeant said.
'I've drunk 'is beer a score o' times,' said Files-on-Parade.
''E's drinkin' bitter beer alone,' the Colour-Sergeant said.
They are hangin' Danny Deever, you must mark 'im to 'is place,
For 'e shot a comrade sleepin'—you must look 'im in the face;
Nine 'undred of 'is county an' the Regiment's disgrace,
While they're hangin' Danny Deever in the mornin'.

'What's that so black agin the sun?' said Files-on-Parade.
'It's Danny fightin' 'ard for life,' the Colour-Sergeant said.
'What's that that whimpers over'ead?' said Files-on-Parade.
'It's Danny's soul that's passin' now,' the Colour-Sergeant said.
For they're done with Danny Deever, you can 'ear the quickstep play,
The Regiment's in column, an' they're marchin' us away;
Ho! the young recruits are shakin', an' they'll want their beer to-day,
After hangin' Danny Deever in the mornin'!

HARP SONG OF
THE DANE WOMEN

What is a woman that you forsake her,
And the hearth-fire and the home-acre,
To go with the old grey Widow-maker?

She has no house to lay a guest in—
But one chill bed for all to rest in,
That the pale suns and the stray bergs nest in.

She has no strong white arms to fold you,
But the ten-times-fingering weed to hold you—
Out on the rocks where the tide has rolled you.

Yet, when the signs of summer thicken,
And the ice breaks, and the birch-buds quicken,
Yearly you turn from our side, and sicken—

Sicken again for the shouts and the slaughters.
You steal away to the lapping waters,
And look at your ship in her winter-quarters.

You forget our mirth, and talk at the tables,
The kine in the shed and the horse in the stables—
To pitch her sides and go over her cables.

Then you drive out where the storm-clouds swallow,
And the sound of your oar-blades, falling hollow,
Is all we have left through the months to follow.

Ah, what is Woman that you forsake her,
And the hearth-fire and the home-acre,
To go with the old grey Widow-maker?

MANDALAY

By the old Moulmein Pagoda, lookin' lazy at the sea,
There's a Burma girl a-settin', and I know she thinks o' me;
For the wind is in the palm-trees, and the temple-bells they say:
"Come you back, you British soldier; come you back to Mandalay!"
Come you back to Mandalay,
Where the old Flotilla lay:
Can't you 'ear their paddles chunkin' from Rangoon to Mandalay?
On the road to Mandalay,
Where the flyin'-fishes play,
An' the dawn comes up like thunder outer China 'crost the Bay!

'Er petticoat was yaller an' 'er little cap was green,
An' 'er name was Supi-yaw-lat — jes' the same as Theebaw's Queen,
An' I seed her first a-smokin' of a whackin' white cheroot,
An' a-wastin' Christian kisses on an 'eathen idol's foot:
Bloomin' idol made o'mud —
Wot they called the Great Gawd Budd —
Plucky lot she cared for idols when I kissed 'er where she stud!
On the road to Mandalay . . .

When the mist was on the rice-fields an' the sun was droppin' slow,
She'd git 'er little banjo an' she'd sing "~Kulla-lo-lo!~"
With 'er arm upon my shoulder an' 'er cheek agin' my cheek
We useter watch the steamers an' the ~hathis~ pilin' teak.
Elephints a-pilin' teak
In the sludgy, squdgy creek,
Where the silence 'ung that 'eavy you was 'arf afraid to speak!
On the road to Mandalay . . .

But that's all shove be'ind me — long ago an' fur away,
An' there ain't no 'busses runnin' from the Bank to Mandalay;
An' I'm learnin' 'ere in London what the ten-year soldier tells:
"If you've 'eard the East a-callin', you won't never 'eed naught else."
  No! you won't 'eed nothin' else
  But them spicy garlic smells,
   An' the sunshine an' the palm-trees an' the tinkly temple-bells;
  On the road to Mandalay . . .

I am sick o' wastin' leather on these gritty pavin'-stones,
An' the blasted Henglish drizzle wakes the fever in my bones;
Tho' I walks with fifty 'ousemaids outer Chelsea to the Strand,
An' they talks a lot o' lovin', but wot do they understand?
  Beefy face an' grubby 'and —
  Law! wot do they understand?
   I've a neater, sweeter maiden in a cleaner, greener land!
  On the road to Mandalay . . .

Ship me somewheres east of Suez, where the best is like the worst,
Where there aren't no Ten Commandments an' a man can raise a thirst;
For the temple-bells are callin', an' it's there that I would be —
By the old Moulmein Pagoda, looking lazy at the sea;
  On the road to Mandalay,
  Where the old Flotilla lay,
   With our sick beneath the awnings when we went to Mandalay!
  On the road to Mandalay,
  Where the flyin'-fishes play,
   An' the dawn comes up like thunder outer China 'crost the Bay!

THE WINNERS

1888

WHAT is the moral? Who rides may read.
   When the night is thick and the tracks are blind
A friend at a pinch is a friend indeed,
   But a fool to wait for the laggard behind.
Down to Gehenna or up to the Throne,
   He travels the fastest who travels alone.

White hands cling to the tightened rein,
   Slipping the spur from the booted heel,
Tenderest voices cry'"Turn again,"
   Red lips tarnish the scabbarded steel,
High hopes faint on a warm hearth stone—
   He travels the fastest who travels alone.

One may fall but he falls by himself—
   Falls by himself with himself to blame.
One may attain and to him is pelf—
   Loot of the city in Gold or Fame.
Plunder of earth shall be all his own
   Who travels the fastest and travels alone.

Wherefore the more ye be holpen and stayed—
   Stayed by a friend in the hour of toil,
Sing the heretical song I have made—
   His be the labour and yours be the spoil.
Win by his aid and the aid disown—
   He travels the fastest who travels alone!

BIBLIOGRAPHY

GUNGA DIN,
First published in the *New York Tribune, May 22nd,* 1890

IF—,
Written as a tribute to Leander Starr Jameson, circa
1895. First published in *Rewards and Fairies,* 1910

RECESSIONAL,
First published in *The Times, July 17th,* 1897, shortly followed
by *The Spectator, July 24th* and *The Critic July 31st.*

THE GODS OF THE COPYBOOK HEADINGS,
First published in the *Sunday Pictorial, October
26th* 1919. In America, the title was altered to *The
Gods of the Copybook Margins* and first published
in *Harper's Magazine, January,* 1920

THE WHITE MAN'S BURDEN,
First published in *The Times, February 4th,* 1899
aswell as *Literature* (same day) and followed by
the *New York Tribune, February 5th,* 1899

MESOPOTAMIA,
First published in both the *Morning Post* and the
New York Times, July 11th, 1917. It was rejected
by the *Daily Telegraph* for being too"hard-hitting"
before it was accepted by the *Morning Post.*

THE FEMALE OF THE SPECIES,
First published in the *Morning Post, October* 21*st*, 1911

THE BALLAD OF EAST AND WEST,
First published in the *Pioneer December* 2*nd*, 1889.
The title was originally *Kamal* and was attributed to
Yussuf, one of the pen-names used by Kipling.

EPITAPHS OF THE WAR,
First published in *The Years Between*, 1919

THE WAY THROUGH THE WOODS,
First published in *Rewards and Fairies*, 1910

MOTHER O' MINE,
First published in The Light That Failed, 1892 as a dedication.

TOMMY,
First published in the *Scot's Observer March*
1*st*, 1890 and *St. James's Gazette* (same day).
Orginally titled *The Queen's Uniform*

THE GLORY OF THE GARDEN,
First published in *A School History of England*, 1911

DANNY DEEVER,
First published in the *Scot's Observer February* 22*nd*, 1890

HARP SONG OF THE DANE WOMEN,
First published in *Puck of Pook's Hill*, 1906 for
the story *The Knights of the Joyous Venture*

MANDALAY
First published in the *Scot's Observer June* 21*st*, 1890

THE BEST OF RUDYARD KIPLING

THE WINNERS,
First published in *The Indian Railway Library, Volume 2*, 1888. The poem was originally called *L'Envoi* and was an introduction to the story *The Story of the Gadsbys*. It was also published in the first English edition of *Soldiers Three* in the same year.